NATURE'S CHILDREN™

AARDVARKS

by Josh Gregory

Children's Press®

An Imprint of Scholastic Inc.
New York   Toronto   London   Auckland   Sydney
Mexico City   New Delhi   Hong Kong
Danbury, Connecticut

Content Consultant
Dr. Stephen S. Ditchkoff
Professor of Wildlife Sciences
Auburn University
Auburn, Alabama

Photographs ©: Alamy Images: 22, 23 (David Keith Jones); 1, 2, 3, 20, 21, 46 (Schmidbauer); Corbis Images: 5 bottom, 40, 41 (Laurin Schmid), 32 (Shaen Adey), 28, 29 (VidiPhoto); Dreamstime: 2, 3 background, 44-45 background (Annemario), 36, 37 (Clickit); Everett Collection: 16 (David Hosking), 31 (Rex USA); Getty Images/ wendy salisbury: cover; Media Bakery: 6, 7 (Frans Lanting), 8, 9 (Nigel Dennis); National Geographic Creative/Beverly Joubert: 15; Newscom/Anthony Bannister: 12; Science Source/David Hosking: 38, 39; Shutterstock, Inc.: 34, 35 (Greg Amptman), 18, 19 (Klanarong Chitmung); Superstock, Inc.: 4, 5 background, 10, 11 (age fotostock), 26, 27 (Biosphoto); Thinkstock/Eric Isselée: 5 top, 24.

Library of Congress Cataloging-in-Publication Data
Gregory, Josh, author.
  Aardvarks / by Josh Gregory.
      pages cm. — (Nature's children)
  Summary: "This book details the life and habits of aardvarks."— Provided by publisher.
  Audience: Ages 9–12.
  Audience: Grades 4 to 6.
  Includes bibliographical references and index.
  ISBN 978-0-531-21166-3 (library binding) —
  ISBN 978-0-531-21185-4 (pbk.)
  1. Aardvark—Juvenile literature. I. Title. II. Series: Nature's children (New York, N.Y.)
  QL737.T8G74 2015
  599.3'1—dc23   2014029895

Printed in China 62
SCHOLASTIC, CHILDREN'S PRESS, and associated logos are trademarks and/or registered trademarks of Scholastic Inc.

1 2 3 4 5 6 7 8 9 10 R 24 23 22 21 20 19 18 17 16 15

Aardvarks

Class	Mammalia
Order	Tubulidentata
Family	Orycteropodidae
Genus	*Orycteropus*
Species	*Orycteropus afer*
World distribution	Sub-Saharan Africa
Habitats	Savannas, grasslands, forests
Distinctive physical characteristics	Long snout; small eyes and large ears; long, thick claws; roughly 3 to 5 feet (0.9 to 1.5 meters) long, with a 2-foot (0.6 m) tail; weighs roughly 85 to 150 pounds (39 to 68 kilograms); covered in a thin coat of grayish and sometimes brownish hair; face and tip of tail are lighter color
Habits	Sleeps in burrows during the day and emerges at night to forage for food; uses powerful claws to open insect mounds and long face and tongue to reach inside; mainly solitary; usually gives birth to a single offspring once per year; digs to escape from predators; uses claws to fend off attackers if necessary
Diet	Primarily ants, termites, and other insects; occasionally eats cucumbers as a source of water

Contents

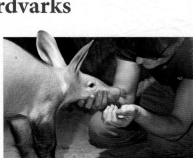

CHAPTER 1

Night Foragers

A light breeze blows through the bushes as the sun sets on the African savanna. It was a hot, bright afternoon, but the air is beginning to cool as the sun drops below the horizon. Some of the savanna's animals are settling down to sleep for the night. For many others, however, the day is just beginning.

A small cloud of dust rises into the air as a nearby patch of dirt begins to shift. Before long, the dirt patch has opened up to reveal a tunnel entrance. A long, narrow face pokes out of the hole and sniffs at the air. It is an aardvark emerging from its burrow to begin its nightly foraging. After making sure the coast is clear, the aardvark leaps forward out of the hole and begins hopping around. It pauses to once again search its surroundings for danger, and then moves off into the night to find something to eat.

Aardvarks are very cautious as they leave their underground homes at night.

Earth Pigs

In the Afrikaans language of South Africa, the word *aardvark* means "earth pig." Though aardvarks are not actually pigs, it is easy to see how they got their name. An aardvark's long, narrow snout ends in a flat nose that resembles a pig's. Beneath this nose is a small mouth. Aardvarks also have small, dark eyes and long, rabbit-like ears. Their round bodies are covered in a sparse coat of gray and sometimes brownish fur. On many aardvarks, the fur on the face and tip of the tail is almost white.

An aardvark has four muscular legs. Each of its front feet has four toes, and each of its back feet has five. These toes end in flat, shovel-shaped claws.

A fully grown aardvark weighs roughly 85 to 150 pounds (39 to 68 kilograms). Its body is around 3 to 5 feet (0.9 to 1.5 meters) long, with a 2-foot (0.6 m) tail.

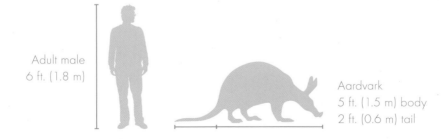

Adult male
6 ft. (1.8 m)

Aardvark
5 ft. (1.5 m) body
2 ft. (0.6 m) tail

Some aardvarks have darker fur than others.

African Animals

Wild aardvarks can thrive in many different environments. They live throughout the huge portion of the African continent that lies south of the Sahara Desert. They have a fairly wide range, and Africa is home to a wide variety of habitats.

As long as there are plenty of insects to eat and places to dig burrows, aardvarks can live comfortably. They are most common in Africa's wide stretches of savanna and grassland environments. They sometimes live in forests as well. Aardvarks avoid living in areas where the soil is extremely hard or rocky, as this makes it difficult for them to dig underground. They also tend to avoid regions that experience flooding. The water could easily leak into their burrows and drown them.

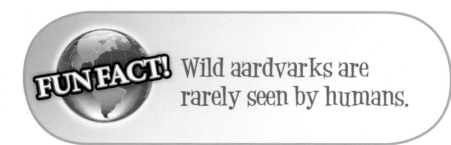

FUN FACT! Wild aardvarks are rarely seen by humans.

Tall grass helps aardvarks keep the entrances to their burrows hidden from enemies.

12

Digging Deep

Burrows are an extremely important part of an aardvark's life. Aardvarks dig their homes into the ground using their large, strong claws. Most aardvark burrows are simple tunnels with a single entrance. Usually, these burrows are roughly 6 to 10 feet (1.8 to 3 m) deep. However, some burrows are far more complex. They might extend as far as 20 feet (6 m) beneath the surface and contain up to 43 feet (13 m) of tunnels. A number of sleeping chambers may branch off from the tunnels, and the burrow might have several entrances. Aardvarks usually plug up these entrances, leaving only small holes to serve as air vents. This helps prevent **predators** from getting inside their homes. Aardvarks do not live in the same burrow for long periods of time. Instead, they move to new areas and dig new burrows often.

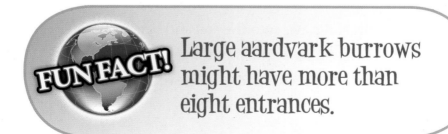

FUN FACT! Large aardvark burrows might have more than eight entrances.

The tunnels in a burrow are just wide enough for an aardvark to move through them.

CHAPTER 2

An Aardvark's Abilities

The aardvark is sometimes called the antbear. This nickname comes from the aardvark's incredible appetite for its favorite food—insects, especially ants and termites. A hungry aardvark can eat as many as 50,000 insects during a single night of foraging. Though its diet consists almost entirely of ants and termites, it sometimes eats other types of insects as well.

Ants and termites live inside mounds of dirt. These mounds can be almost as hard as rocks, which offers the insects protection from many potential predators. However, aardvarks are perfectly equipped to tear these obstacles apart and reach the insects inside. When an aardvark locates a mound full of termites or ants, it plunges its powerful claws into the soil and begins digging. Once it creates an opening in the mound, it can stick its long snout and sticky tongue inside and begin feasting.

A termite mound might look like a simple pile of dirt, but it is filled with thousands of insects.

Mighty Mouths

Thanks to its remarkable snout and tongue, an aardvark can eat a huge number of insects very quickly. The snout's long, narrow shape allows it to fit into tight spaces, so the aardvark does not need to completely destroy an insect mound to eat. As the aardvark sticks its snout into a mound, it opens its mouth and extends its long, sticky tongue into the mound's tunnels and chambers. An aardvark's tongue can be as long as 12 inches (30 centimeters). Insects become stuck to it, and the aardvark pulls these insects into its mouth.

An aardvark's teeth are unlike any other animal's. Each tooth is formed from a large number of tube-shaped structures packed closely together. These teeth grow continually throughout an aardvark's life, and they are worn down as the aardvark chews. As a result, the teeth have a mostly flat shape. This makes them perfect for grinding up mouthfuls of crunchy insects.

An aardvark's snout and tongue allow it to reach deep into insect burrows.

Tough Enough

Even though the insects that make up an aardvark's diet are very small, they have powerful ways of defending themselves against most predators. If an insect has ever bitten or stung you, then you've experienced these defenses firsthand. Many insects produce dangerous venom that can cause serious injury or even death to large animals. Insects that live in large groups, including ants and termites, can swarm onto their enemies, biting or stinging them hundreds of times.

Aardvarks have built-in defenses against insect attacks. These defenses enable them to dive into an insect mound without fear. An aardvark's main protection is its extremely tough, thick skin. Insect bites or stings cannot pierce it, so the attacks cause no harm to the aardvark. Aardvarks can also close off their nostrils to prevent insects from swarming inside, where they might find a vulnerable place to bite.

An ant's powerful jaws are no match for an aardvark's defenses.

Observing the World

Aardvarks have extremely sharp senses that help them locate prey while avoiding predators and other threats. Aardvarks search for insects primarily by sniffing and touching the ground. They have a tremendous sense of smell. In fact, the part of their brain that processes smells is so large that the skull bulges outward slightly in the center of the aardvark's head. As a result, aardvarks can sniff at the dirt and smell insects that are underground. Aardvarks also have special organs in their snouts that enable them to feel very slight vibrations. As they press their noses against the ground, they can feel insects moving around beneath the surface.

Aardvarks do not have strong vision. They can see in the dark, but they cannot detect color very well. As a result, they must rely heavily on their excellent hearing to notice threats approaching. Each of their long ears can move separately from the other. This allows an aardvark to listen in multiple directions without moving its head.

Aardvarks almost always keep their noses near the ground as they walk around.

Making a Move

Aardvarks mostly get around by walking. They are good swimmers, but they rarely have any need to use this skill. Aardvarks can run fairly quickly when they are in danger, but their short legs keep them from being truly excellent runners. Instead, they are at their speediest when they are digging. It can take as little as five minutes for an aardvark to dig a hole large enough to fit its entire body inside!

An aardvark digs by using its claws to scoop out dirt and push it backward. Dirt from the front claws is pushed backward to the rear legs, which kick the dirt behind the aardvark's body. An aardvark can fold its ears shut and close its nostrils while digging, to keep them from filling with dirt. This means it can dive headfirst into the dirt and disappear underground in a matter of minutes.

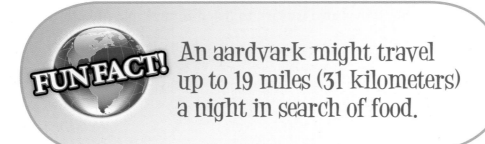

FUN FACT! An aardvark might travel up to 19 miles (31 kilometers) a night in search of food.

Dirt flies out from behind an aardvark's rear legs as it digs a burrow.

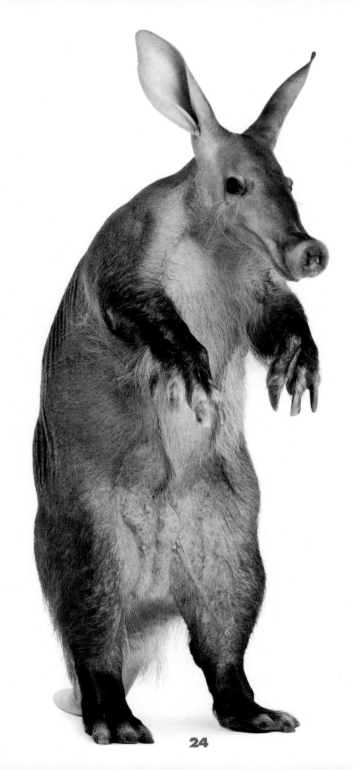

Flee or Fight

Aardvarks must always stay on the lookout for dangerous predators when they are aboveground. The savannas, grasslands, and forests of Africa are home to some of the most fearsome animal **species** on Earth. Huge, powerful cats such as lions and leopards are among the aardvark's most common predators. Pythons and hyenas are also known to hunt aardvarks.

When an aardvark notices that a predator is nearby, its best defense is to run away and dig a burrow as quickly as possible. However, there is not always enough time to escape underground. In these cases, an aardvark must do its best to fight off the attacker. The aardvark often rears up onto its back legs, using its tail for balance. It can then swipe at its enemy using its dangerous front claws. Other times, the aardvark might roll onto its back and kick at a predator with all four feet.

An aardvark can be a strong fighter when it stands on its hind legs.

CHAPTER 3

Lonely Lifestyle

Aardvarks are not very social animals. In areas where there are a large number of aardvarks, two or three of them might share the same burrow. However, this is not common. Instead, aardvarks usually prefer to live alone and spend almost all of their time on their own.

An aardvark usually sleeps through the daylight hours underground, where it is sheltered from the hot, sunny weather that is common in its habitat. At night, the aardvark emerges from its burrow and performs a jumping behavior before setting off for the area where it will forage for food. Foraging areas are not always in the same location as the burrow, and the aardvark might have to travel several miles to find food each night. As daylight approaches, the aardvark journeys back to its burrow to sleep.

Aardvarks spend much of their time resting in the sleeping chambers of their burrows.

Meeting a Mate

Adult aardvarks spend time together only during their yearly mating season. This period falls at different times of the year depending on where the aardvarks live. Aardvarks found in southern Africa tend to mate sometime between October and December. Those in the northern part of the continent are more likely to mate in March or April.

During mating season, male aardvarks produce musk. Females who are ready to mate smell the musk and seek out the males. After mating, the male and female go their separate ways. Once the female is pregnant, she does not seek out other mates. Male aardvarks, however, might mate with several different females during a single mating season. Around seven months after mating, the female gives birth to a single offspring.

Zookeepers watch as a pair of aardvarks socializes at a zoo in the Netherlands.

Bringing Up Baby

Baby aardvarks look much like adults when they are born. However, they are much smaller, weighing only about 4.4 pounds (2 kg). They have wrinkled skin and no hair.

A newborn aardvark stays hidden away in the safety of its mother's den until it is about two weeks old. Around this time, it begins following its mother outside as she forages for insects at night. However, the baby does not start eating insects itself until it is around three months old. Until then, it survives by drinking milk from its mother.

By the time an aardvark is around six months old, its mother is ready to mate again, so the young aardvark becomes independent. At around two years old, it can begin mating and producing babies of its own. In the wild, an aardvark lives to be around 18 years old. Aardvarks in captivity usually live several years longer.

Baby aardvarks are very playful.

CHAPTER 4

Yesterday and Today

Aardvarks are unique animals. Even though they share similarities with many other mammals, they have very few close relatives. They are the only living species in the order Tubulidentata. The name of this order comes from the Latin words for "tube teeth," and it refers to the structure of the aardvark's teeth.

Though the aardvark is the only tube-toothed animal living today, other Tubulidentata species roamed Earth millions of years ago. These ancestors occupied a far wider range than today's aardvarks. Fossils show that tube-toothed animals once lived in what are now Europe, Asia, and the Middle East. Fossils also indicate that Tubulidentata species have existed for at least 54 million years. Scientists believe that some of these extinct ancestors lived very differently from modern aardvarks. They think these creatures may have been poor diggers and ate more plants than insects.

An ancient rock painting depicts an aardvark.

Living Relatives

An aardvark's closest living relatives might come as a surprise. If you look at an aardvark's ears, you might think that it is related to a rabbit. Its nose looks a lot like a pig's. Its long face, claws, and diet might make the aardvark seem like a close cousin of the anteater. However, these animals are not close relatives at all. Aardvarks actually have a much closer genetic similarity to elephants, manatees, dugongs, and hyraxes.

Elephants are the largest land animals living today. They are found throughout many parts of Africa and Asia. Like aardvarks, they have very thick skin. Manatees and dugongs are large aquatic mammals. Manatees are found mainly along coastal areas of the Atlantic Ocean, while dugongs live in the Indian and Pacific Oceans. Hyraxes are small, furry animals that look a lot like rodents. Like elephants, they are found in parts of Africa and Asia. Unlike aardvarks, all of these animals are herbivores.

Though they don't look much alike, manatees and aardvarks are closely related.

CHAPTER 5

Living with Aardvarks

Like all wild plant and animal species, aardvarks play an important part in keeping their ecosystem healthy. One important benefit of having aardvarks in an area is that their burrows provide shelter for other animal species. When an aardvark moves on to a new burrow, a different animal can take over the old burrow. Wild dogs and warthogs are some of the larger animals known to occupy abandoned aardvark burrows. Squirrels, bats, and even certain bird species also make homes in aardvark burrows.

Aardvarks also keep insect populations from growing too large in certain areas. This is especially helpful to humans. Termites and ants can reproduce very quickly. Large groups of them can damage crops and buildings. By eating many of these insects every day, aardvarks keep them from becoming too numerous.

Aardvark burrows make perfect homes for animals, such as warthogs, that are unable to dig their own holes.

Human Threats

While lions, leopards, and other predators are all fearsome hunters, an aardvark's biggest threat is actually humans. Humans kill aardvarks for a number of reasons. Some people hunt them as a source of meat. Others kill them to use their skin, teeth, and claws to make decorative objects. Some people believe that parts of the aardvark have healing properties.

Aardvarks are most often killed because humans see their burrows as a nuisance. When an aardvark digs a tunnel underground, the soil above is weakened. If a heavy object such as a vehicle or a tractor drives over the top of the burrow, the soil can collapse. This can damage the vehicle and possibly injure the driver or passengers. As a result, some farmers and ranchers kill any aardvarks they find on their property. This has led to aardvarks being completely wiped out in certain areas.

Aardvarks' digging can create dangers for humans who live nearby.

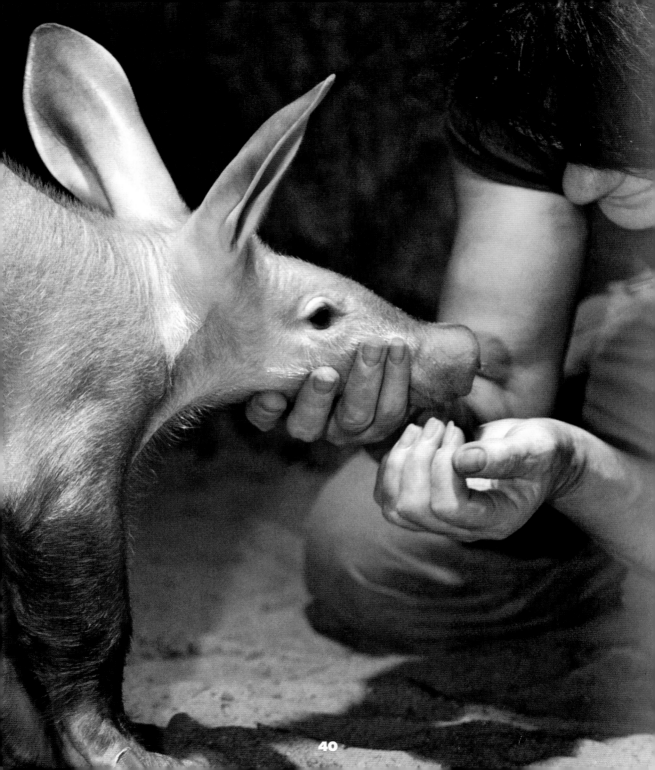

Looking Forward

Aardvarks are also harmed indirectly by many widespread human activities. For example, most modern farmers rely on chemicals called pesticides to keep insects from damaging their crops. The farmers spray these poisonous chemicals on their plants, and any insects that get too close are killed. Unfortunately, killing this many insects can greatly reduce available food sources for nearby aardvarks.

Aardvarks are also affected by habitat loss. As humans clear natural land to use for farming, building houses, and various activities, there is less space for aardvarks and other wild animals to live. Climate change could have a major effect on the future survival of aardvarks and other species, too.

Aardvarks are not endangered. However, it is still important to treat them with respect. By keeping the needs of wild animals and the rest of the natural world in mind, we can make sure that these incredible animals will continue to thrive for generations to come.

Wildlife experts help make sure that aardvarks stay healthy.

Words to Know

ancestors (AN-ses-turz) — ancient animal species that are related to modern species

aquatic (uh-KWAH-tik) — living or growing in water

burrow (BUR-oh) — a tunnel or a hole in the ground made or used as a home by a rabbit or other animal

captivity (kap-TIV-i-tee) — the condition of being held or trapped by people

climate change (KLYE-mit CHAYNJ) — global warming and other changes in the weather and weather patterns that are happening because of human activity

ecosystem (EE-koh-sis-tuhm) — all the living things in a place and their relation to the environment

endangered (en-DAYN-jurd) — at risk of becoming extinct, usually because of human activity

foraging (FOR-ij-ing) — searching for food

fossils (FAH-suhlz) — bones, shells, or other traces of an animal or plant from millions of years ago, preserved as rock

genetic (juh-NET-ik) — having to do with the personal characteristics that are passed from parents to their young

habitats (HAB-uh-tats) — places where an animal or a plant is usually found

herbivores (HUR-buh-vorz) — animals that only eat plants

mammals (MAM-uhlz) — warm-blooded animals that have hair or fur and usually give birth to live babies; female mammals produce milk to feed their young

mating (MAYT-ing) — joining together to produce babies

musk (MUHSK) — a substance with a strong smell to attract mates

order (OR-duhr) — a category that groups different families of animals together according to similar traits that they share

pesticides (PES-ti-sydz) — chemicals used to kill pests, such as insects

predators (PREH-duh-turz) — animals that live by hunting other animals for food

prey (PRAY) — an animal that's hunted by another animal for food

range (RAYNJ) — the overall area where an animal can be found

rodents (ROH-duhnts) — mammals with large, sharp front teeth that are constantly growing and used for gnawing things

species (SPEE-sheez) — one of the groups into which animals and plants of the same genus are divided; members of the same species can mate and have offspring

swarm (SWORM) — to move closely together, forming a dense mass

venom (VEH-num) — poison produced by some animals

Habitat Map

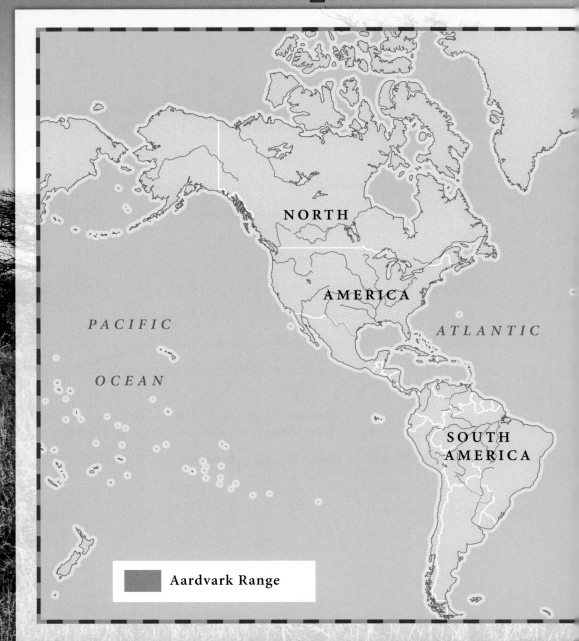

NORTH

AMERICA

PACIFIC

OCEAN

ATLANTIC

SOUTH
AMERICA

Aardvark Range

ARCTIC OCEAN

EUROPE

ASIA

AFRICA

PACIFIC OCEAN

OCEAN

INDIAN OCEAN

AUSTRALIA

Find Out More

Books

Borgert-Spaniol, Megan. *Aardvarks*. Minneapolis: Bellwether Media, 2014.

Gibbs, Maddie. *Aardvarks*. New York: PowerKids Press, 2011.

Visit this Scholastic Web site for more information on aardvarks:
www.factsfornow.scholastic.com
Enter the keyword **Aardvarks**

Index

Page numbers in *italics* indicate a photograph or map.

(Index continued)

About the Author

Josh Gregory writes and edits books for kids. He lives in Chicago, Illinois.